The Church and Identity Theft

WANDA CONWAY-ANTOINE

The Church and Identity Theft

Wanda Conway-Antoine

Kravitz & Sons

INNOVATORS IN PUBLISHING, MARKETING AND ADVERTISING

Kravitz and Sons LLC
204 E Arlington Blvd. Suite B
Greenville, NC 27858

Published by Kravitz and Sons LLC.

ISBN: 979-8-89639-800-4 (sc)
ISBN: 979-8-89639-801-1 (e)

Because of the dynamic nature of the Internet, any web addresses or links contained in this book may have changed since publication and may no longer be valid. The views expressed in this work are solely those of the author and do not necessarily reflect the views of the publisher, and the publisher hereby disclaims any responsibility for them.

Table of Contents

Dedication

To Him who in Christ always leads us in *triumph* and through us spreads the fragrance of the knowledge of Him everywhere. Thank you, Father, for Your faithfulness and truth, which is my shield and my buckler.

Acknowledgments

I would like to acknowledge my husband, Rickey Antoine, for his unending support and encouragement and for having faith in my faith in the Lord Jesus. I love you!

Venessa Harris for her amazing support, her suggestions, for truly reading this work and most of all for her encouragement to go forward.

Thank you guys for everything…

Introduction

The enemy deceives many to use the name of Jesus without His permission.

> …having on His head a golden crown, and in His hand a sharp sickle…Thrust in Your sickle and reap, for the time has come for You to reap, for the harvest of the earth is ripe.
> Revelation 14:14-15 (NKJV)

We grow closer and closer to the manifestation of Jesus' return on the white cloud. Our Lord in heaven has appointed soldiers and ambassadors of Jesus Christ at this dispensation of time to shine the light of the gospel on those who have been deceived by the enemy and allowed him to use them to participate in *identity theft*—unauthorized use of the name of Jesus.

Let me start now by sharing what the Lord has to say about the biggest and fastest-growing lie in recent history by Satan and his demons. In doing this, I will draw your thoughts to a natural crime called "identity theft." Many have fallen prey to this crime and others are doing whatever they can to prevent it from happening to them. At the same time, there are still those who have heard about it but are not very concerned and take no real precautions against it. This is usually because they don't think it will happen to them for several reasons.

One morning while going through treatment for cancer, I was meditating and praying to the Lord about how He could be glorified through this experience. During this time, I was compelled to examine my relationship with Jesus and His purpose for my life. I knew the Lord had given me the ability to write and the gift to teach His word but I did not know how He might use this experience to glorify Himself. There are so many books about cancer and I did not feel He was leading me to write about my cancer experience. After some time and not hearing from the Lord, I decided to go through my mail. I came upon an advertisement for identity theft insurance. As I was about to toss it into the junk mail stack, the phrase, *identity theft* caught my attention. Immediately, the Lord began to impress upon me how Satan uses a similar spiritual tactic to steal the name of Jesus and its benefits. Consequently, there is active *identity theft* present in the body of Christ. The church has, over a period of time, systematically allowed and inadvertently encouraged the use of the name of Jesus without the permission or authority of the Savior Himself. The church has not just allowed this to happen but has become so resigned to it that it can no longer recognize this theft or its effect on the body of Christ.

As you read this book, I encourage you to keep an open mind, an open heart, and open ears. If you would, pray even now that

> ...the God of our Lord Jesus Christ, the Father of glory, may give to you the spirit of wisdom and revelation in the knowledge of Him, the eyes of your understanding being enlightened; that you may know what is the hope of His calling.
> Ephesians 1:17-18 (NKJV)

I trust that He will allow you to see that unless the church takes seriously the responsibility given it by the Lord Jesus, it will, without knowledge or intent, continue to participate in the eternal destruction of many who call themselves Christians.

It is my prayer that this book will accomplish all that the Lord has sent it forth to accomplish. I stand on the word of God that says, *"So shall My Word be that goes forth from My mouth, It shall not return to Me void, but shall accomplish what I please"* (Isaiah 55:11, NKJV). While I am a little apprehensive about writing this, I am honored because the Lord Jesus has found me a usable vessel for this service. I am apprehensive because what this message reveals will go against a lot of what is being taught and tolerated in the church today. Quite frankly, I am just so thankful that this is the Lord's battle, leaving me only responsible for obeying Him. Bottom line, this book is for His glory, His purpose, and for our good. Honor and glory to the Most High God, for He is good and his mercy endures forever!

As we consider the following message, we will see that Satan is still a liar, a thief, and a destroyer. The good news is that he, Satan, is still defeated and Jesus is exalted and is once again exemplified as our Lord brings to light this move of the enemy.

In this written work, we will consider the cunning tactics of the enemy, the church's response to the great commission, the church's irresponsibility in *identity theft* as it relates to the name of Jesus, the promise of the witness of the Holy Spirit, the Lord's insurance against this theft, and the sufficiency of God's grace to overcome its affect.

As the Lord opens this up to His church, we will find that this revelation is not shared for mere information or minimal consideration, but it is for the sake of the gospel of Jesus Christ! It is written for the purpose of bringing to our memory, *"the truth which God has shown in our hearts to give the light of the knowledge of the glory of God in the face of Jesus"* (2 Corinthians 4:6, NKJV). I challenge you to come back and read this statement again after you have completed this book. If you will read this book with an open heart and a desire to hear from the Lord, it will illuminate what you read from this point forward.

I can hear the Lord saying, Turn from working out of natural love and return to me and my way, the God of true love. My love for the world surpasses all understanding. It is an everlasting love that is complete and without compromise. Stop and know that *"I am the same today, yesterday and forever."* (Hebrew 13:8, NKJV) The Word of God does not change. In fact, the Lord says, *"Heaven and earth will pass away, but My words will by no means pass away"* (Matthew 24:35, NKJV). God's great love for the world and His tender mercy and amazing grace inspires this book to reach out to those who are ignorantly using the name of Jesus without a relationship with Him. He desires that we examine ourselves and examine the authenticity of our faith and our knowledge of the Lord, but just as important, His knowledge of us. Do this and we will *not* be among those who say, *"Lord, Lord, have we not prophesied in Your name…"* (Matthew 7:22, NKJV). Instead, we will become the church for which our Savior suffered and died. We will be beneficiaries of the prayer that Jesus prayed in John 17: *"…that they all may be one, as You, Father, are in Me, and I in You; that they also may be one is Us, that the world may believe that You sent Me"* (John 17:21, NKJV).

I am excited because I believe that there will be some who will read these words and be made glad in their hearts because not only do they know the Lord Jesus, but also the Lord Jesus knows them. I am also excited because there will be some who read these words and will seek and accept the revelation of Jesus Christ as they, for the first time, invite the

Lord Jesus into their hearts to become Lord of their lives. At this time, they will become authentic believers as well as authorized, Holy Spirit filled users of the "Name of Jesus."

Identity Theft:

Using the Name of Jesus Without His Permission

> Not everyone who says to Me, "Lord, Lord" shall enter the kingdom of heaven, but he who does the will of my Father in heaven. Many will say to Me in that day, "Lord, Lord, have we not prophesied in Your name, cast out demons in Your name, and done many wonders in Your name?" And then I will declare to them, "I never knew you; depart from Me, you who practice lawlessness."
> Matthew 7:21-23 (RSV)

Identity theft is when someone steals identifying information belonging to another person. This theft is committed with the intention of using the victim's name and other information in order to profit in cash or unauthorized purchases. Subsequently, the thief now has possession of items, often cash without the right to possess. Many times the financial consequences of this crime become the responsibility of the victim.

The progress in technology by way of online shopping and credit card purchases makes this a very prevalent and attractive crime. As the creativity and ingenuity of man make leaps and bounds toward more conveniences, so does the rise in greed and laziness show itself in the world's system. These conveniences find their way into the ministry of the church. The church no longer relies on the gospel of

Christ alone to multiply the church. It, for the purpose and goal of growth, conforms progressively to the ways of the world. As it does this, it opens itself to the same possibilities of deceit and carelessness.

There are several points that will be considered as it relates to *identity theft* within the church of Jesus Christ. The first point to note is that there is intentional and unintentional unauthorized use of the name of Jesus. In America particularly, the Christian faith has been diluted to a social club where 'good things are done'. It has even been perverted to justify all kinds of atrocities. It seems to have become popular and appropriate for social purposes as well as other reasons that have nothing to do with the grace and love of God, the Father.

I knew an Asian man several years ago that came to America from China. He was very intelligent and actually received his education here in America. He worked hard studying in order to get the good things America has to offer. He admitted to me that he had been baptized nine times. When I asked why so many times, he revealed that whenever he would move to another city or community, he would go to the nearest church and when the doors of the church were opened, he would go up to profess his faith. Consequently, he would be baptized so that he would be accepted in that particular community. You see, he perceived that being a Christian was necessary to fit in and be accepted by the type of people he wanted to be associated with here in America. While this is one example of intentionally using the name of Jesus without authority, I am sure there are other reasons just as incredible.

There are also those who are sincere in their use of the name of Jesus. However, they have never had the Holy Spirit of God to witness with their spirit that they have been born again. They operate solely on the acceptance of truth in their minds and the affirmation of other believers. This represents Christianity's move from a heart issue to an intellectual belief based on historical proof that Jesus existed. This intellectual proof, however, leaves out the most important truth of all: It is faith that pleases God! It is a heart issue when a person can accept this as truth without any historical proof at all.

This book is not about separating the wheat from the tares—that is the responsibility of our Lord. However, we are talking about those who are deceived into believing that they are of the household of faith and are entitled to the inheritance, which is in heaven for the church of Jesus Christ.

When the name of Jesus is used without his permission, it is the same as *identity theft*. With *identity theft*, usually the thief has enough information about the person to take on the identity of that person while on the other hand the victim usually knows nothing of the person who stole their identity. This is generally what happens when people use the name of Jesus without his permission. The genuine Christian uses the name of Jesus legitimately and with the authority and guarantee of the Holy Spirit of God. I submit that those people who are using our Lord's name without the indwelling of the Holy Spirit of God are committing *"identity theft."*

The Church's Response to Jesus' Command

And He said unto them, Go into all the world
and preach the gospel to every creature. He who
believes and is baptized will be saved; but he that
does not believe will be damned.
Mark 16:15-16 (NKJV)

When Jesus spoke to his followers before His ascension,
He told them to preach the gospel to every creature.
He went on to say that those who believed shall be saved.
Therefore, it is not enough to know the gospel but the gospel
must be believed before it can do its regenerating and mind
renewing work. Consequently, the church must respond to
the mandate of Jesus by sharing the uncompromised gospel.
The same gospel Jesus and the disciples used to multiply
the early church must be used today. When the gospel is
believed in the heart, a born again believer is the result. This
process is shared by God and the church, his fellow workers.
It is written in 1 Corinthians 3:7 that the church plants and
waters but it is God who gives the increase. Therefore, we
are not called to seek ways to lead people to Christ. God
has already made the way and we must trust that His plan
is sufficient.

Now that the gospel has been shared, and a new believer
is born, the church must now respond with teaching by the
power of the Holy Spirit. As a new believer, it is important
to continue in the word of God so that one may become an
effective disciple. In this sense, a disciple is a disciplined one

obeying the commands of Jesus Christ. However, to become a disciple, the believer must know the word of God and obey it.

Often, the church starts with the command of obedience and overlooks the process of being born again. Jesus says, *"Most assuredly, I say to you, unless one is born again, he cannot see the kingdom of God."* John 3:3 (NKJV). When sharing the gospel, the church must no longer replace the spirituality of salvation with intellectual persuasion and historical proof. Jesus told Peter when he said that Jesus was the Christ, the living Son of God, *"Blessed are you Simon Bar-Jonah, for flesh and blood has not revealed this to you, but My Father who is in heaven"*(Matthew 16:17 NKJV). Using one's intellect becomes valuable later in this regenerating experience in order to be able to have an answer for the hope that they now have in Christ Jesus. While to be an effective Christian, intellectualism and spiritualism is mutually necessary, one's walk in true faith in Christ Jesus can not be proven by information and knowledge but by walking in unconditional love for one another. Jesus says, *"By this all will know that you are My disciples, if you have love for one another."* (John 13:35 NKJV). When the church consistently, and with wisdom respond to its call according to the commission given by Jesus, there will be fewer people relying on their intellect and works to gain them a right to the tree of life.

It is the responsibility of the church to present the gospel to the unbeliever according to the unction of the Holy Spirit. There cannot be growth without first planting the seed. We must no longer offer to the unbeliever the fruits of a relationship with Christ Jesus before planting the seed from which this fruit grows. In other words, we cannot continue to lead people to believe that doing the right things, coming to church, and giving are means to gain the right to the tree of life. But instead, we must proclaim the *love of God* through the gospel of Christ and only the gospel of Christ as the way to gain access to the tree of life. These other things will be the fruit of that decision.

It is the responsibility of the church to plant the seed of the gospel and to water that seed, but it is God's responsibility to give that seed increase. Jesus says, *"No one can come to me unless the Father who sent Me draws him; and I will raise him up the last day"* (John 6:44, NKJV). It is clear that it is God, the Father, who will draw men to Christ Jesus.

The Church's Irresponsibility

You are the salt of the earth, but if the salt loses
its flavor, how shall it be seasoned? It is then good
for nothing but to be thrown out and trampled
under foot by men. You are the light of the world.
A city that is set on a hill cannot be hidden. Nor
do they light a lamp and put it under a basket but
on a lamp stand, and it gives light to all who are
in the house. Let your light so shine before men,
that they may see your good works and glorify
your Father in heaven.
Matthew 5:13-16 (NKJV)

Why is it so easy for an identity to be stolen? There are
many cases of identity theft that are caused by companies who are careless with the security of personal information. However, some instances are a result of individuals who are not cautious with the handling of their personal information. For example, we throw away documents such as credit card statements, pre-approved credit offers, and even cancelled checks in the trash that has everything someone needs to steal our identity. We sometimes make our information available to a potential thief unknowingly by giving personal information to unknown persons over the phone, or the internet. It is in these situations that we are acting irresponsibly in handling our personal information.

Now let's look at some ways the church operates irresponsibly when handling the word of God. First, many of us have moved away from the truth that the church belongs to Jesus Christ. We have taken ownership of the church by words and too often by actions. For example, we actually put "founder" by our names when advertising a church family. Oh, of course, we do this for many reasons and it is not because we don't know whose church it is. We believe and teach that our words make a difference in our attitudes and thinking. Would this not be true in all our words? When we say that "This is my church," or "I am the founder of this church," we are not just identifying our church family. Over time, we begin to act like it is *my church.* Before we know it, our attitude exudes this and the crack in which the enemy can enter has been formed. In other words, we have once again become vulnerable to the enemy and his tactics. An increasing occurrence exemplifying this weakness is when a church body seeks the world's legal system for settling its disputes with members or leaders. The local church should be a place where we can feel a personal investment and/or personal admiration, but we must never forget that it is the Lord Jesus' church. We sometimes put so much emphasis on the building and the denomination, remembering that the church is the people eludes us. While there is a place for solidarity within a particular church body, this solidarity must never exclude the importance of the whole church no matter the denomination. As individual members of the body of Christ, we must not condone those in leadership roles who encourage us, even unwittingly, into thinking that our local church family is isolated and somehow special from God's perspective. We can do this when we remember that the word of God tells us that the one who waters and the one who plants is nothing but God who gives the increase. We as members of the body of Christ can turn from this by recognizing that every church door opened in the name of Jesus is part of our family of believers. Focusing on this will make it easier to pray, not only for *my church,* but for the Lord's church. When we lift up the body of Christ as a whole in prayer, it will inevitably exemplify unity in the family of God. Too often we separate ourselves from other memberships because there is no sense of unity within the whole body. Paul prays in Ephesians 4:13, *"Till we all come in the unity of the faith, and of the knowledge of the Son of God, unto a perfect man, unto the measure of the stature of the fulness of Christ:"*

Our distraction when evangelizing to the unbeliever is another act of irresponsibility. We are distracted by the desire to use the right words, fear of rejection, fear of putting our own lives under scrutiny, and yes, we have even left out the true gospel and replaced it with our testimonies of God's goodness . The definition of gospel as used in the Bible is the good news that God in Christ Jesus has fulfilled his promises to Israel, and that a way of salvation has been opened for all.

Recently, I asked several people who I believed to be genuine believers what was the gospel and to give a short summation of it. At least two of the five believers I asked responded with the gospel being that "God is good all the time and He will be with you in troubles; He will never leave you nor forsake you." While these are very true statements, it is not the gospel of Jesus Christ. The true gospel of Jesus Christ can be summed up as follows:

> Everyone has sinned and need a Savior. There is only one who is perfect before God that can fulfill the law completely. Because God, the Father, loves man so much, He sent this perfect man, His son, Jesus, to fulfill the law for all men. In so doing, everyone is forgiven and has a right to the tree of life.
> (John 3:16; Romans 5)

The progress of technology opens the door for more sophisticated crimes. As the world moves forward in its technology, so do people become apathetic in their life choices. As a result, most people look for easy and less costly ways to achieve or attain what they desire. When the church takes this path it leads men to one-sided relationships in the walk of faith. One reason so many people are being deceived into this one-sided relationship leads us to the second point noted in the definition and purpose of *identity theft.*

There are churches that consistently present Christianity as a means of gaining material prosperity as well as a place in heaven, thus enticing the unsaved to seek ways to obtain this promise with little or no commitment on their part. The church must without fail present the truth of God's grace in salvation and his purpose for man's eternal state. When the church makes God's grace for salvation about material prosperity, it inadvertently participates in the enemy's manipulation of the truth. Many in the church lead people who have not recognized and acknowledged their sinful state to believe that going to church will make it possible for them to get that which the world calls valuable. Jesus says, *"seek first the kingdom of God and his righteousness then all these things will be added to you."* (Matthew 6:33 NKJV). When the gospel makes the natural needs of man its focus and all but omit man's need for spiritual regeneration, we are no longer sharing the gospel of Christ. Therefore, without commitment, many are making the profession of Christianity without the cost of submitting to the lordship and commands of our Savior, Jesus Christ.

Who benefits from this deception and who loses? Satan tempted Jesus with food for the natural body and the Lord replied, it is not good for man to live by bread alone but by every word that proceeds from the mouth of God! Satan is the beneficiary of this deception because it has always been his goal to overthrow the kingdom of God. He knows that his time here on earth is quickly coming to an end. Therefore, he seeks to deceive as many as possible before his time is up here. He has always used deception to attain his goal. He did it in the Garden of Eden when he told Eve that she would not surely die if she ate of tree of the knowledge of good and evil. The enemy begins every lie with a bit of truth. He knows that if he includes some truth in his lies, it will make the lie easier to believe. That is how he gets away with so much trickery, which in the end, influences so many well-meaning people. We know that the enemy has always mislead people; however, it seems that he is becoming more and more cunning in these last days. The church is contributing to this deception and does it in the name of God's love. In actuality, it is more in the name of man's natural love and his need to please the masses. We are experiencing the very situation that Paul talks about when he says, *"For the time is coming when people will not endure sound teaching, but having itching ears they will accumulate for themselves teachers to suit their own likings"* (2 Timothy 4:3, NKJV). In the end, those who are deceived are the losers.

Using the name of Jesus without His permission can get your name on the church roll and may even give you a surface confidence about spending eternity in heaven. This confidence, however, does not come from the witnessing of the Holy Spirit to your spirit but from the affirmation of other believers such as those in leadership roles of the church. This does not by any means suggest that affirmation and confirmation is not of value from fellow believers and leaders of the church. What it does mean is that it is necessary, without compromise, that the Holy Spirit be the one in whom you put your trust. It is written, *"The Spirit Himself bears witness with our spirit that we are children of God."* (Romans 8:16 NKJV) The affirmation of others without the witness of the Holy Spirit will not gain entrance into the kingdom of God or a right to the tree of life. According to Matthew 7:21-23, many will be surprised when Jesus sends them away because they trusted in works and in church membership for eternal life. Jesus says, *"it is the Spirit that gives life; the flesh profits nothing. The words that I speak to you are spirit, and they are life."*(John 6:63 NKJV)

Evangelism is the gift God has given the believer to be used for the benefit of the unsaved. When we are evangelizing, we must be proclaiming the love of God through the gospel of Jesus Christ, sharing, and testifying how God the Father sent Jesus to save man from His wrath. The church too rarely shares the true gospel with the unbeliever. This is unacceptable because the gospel is the power of God to salvation.

This gospel must be proclaimed with love and not out of obligation. It is the love of God that will cause men to respond favorably. This love is evident when the gospel is shared at the unction of the Holy Spirit of God. Instead of proclaiming with passion the gospel of Christ, we have taken the gospel of Christ for granted and often times neglect it when we are trying to lead someone to Christ. In our carelessness, the very power that leads someone to saving knowledge of Jesus Christ is completely omitted. It is replaced with invitations to come to church, join church, read the Bible, stop doing this and that, stop sinning, give money, believe in God, etc. This is irresponsible because we who are genuine believers should know that the invitation that the believer should be offering the unsaved first is an invitation to the family of God and not to the meeting place. When offering this invitation there is no specific place that person has to go to receive this gift. Going to the building does not signify membership into God's family. Going to the meeting place of the children of God is what one does to fellowship with other members of the family. It is good to ask someone to experience the family of God if we have first shared the gospel of Christ with that person. Inviting someone to church does not take the place of sharing the awesome gift of grace from God with that person first. While this might seem like a simple case of semantics, it is vital to sharing the true gospel whereby a person can be saved. God used specific *words* to create the heaven, the earth and the fullness therein!

The church, in her attempt to show the love of God has opened the doors of the church's meeting places to all kinds of spirits. A practical definition to distinguish between a natural love and a supernatural love would be that natural love *conditionally seeks to meet the desires* of another while supernatural love *unconditionally meets the need* of the other. Only the love of God is unfailing and pure all the time.

As I study the early church as described in Acts, I see that the church was a place that believers went to be edified and equipped for the task put before it by the Lord Jesus. In fact, it was dangerous for believers to meet publicly. It was customary for them to meet secretly to avoid persecution or even death from those in authority who did not believe. They went out and shared the gospel of Christ with people and then invited them to the meetings. This was dangerous also but I am reminded of a prayer found in Acts 4:23-31 where the disciples prayed after witnessing for Christ and being threatened by the chief priest to never preach the name of Jesus again. They prayed to God for boldness to continue what the Lord had commanded them to do. The bible says, *"and when they had prayed, the place where they were assembled together was shakened, and they were all filled with the Holy Spirit, and they spoke the word of God with boldness"*. (Acts 4:31 NKJV) Their focus was the gospel of Christ and obedience to his command.

In these last days, too often we measure a successful ministry by the number of its members or the number of programs offered. In spite of the large number of followers and the many programs offered, we still ask the question: "Why is there so little power shown in the church these last days?" I am reminded that when the Holy Spirit came as a result of Jesus' promise to the disciples, He came to the more than 120 believers in the upper room. The Bible notes that they were all of one accord in prayer and supplication. (See Acts 1:12-2:4) This makes it clear that when believers are together in one accord, the power of our Lord will show itself. How can we expect to see the power of God in its greatest when we, children of light, are fellowshipping with children of darkness? *"Do not be unequally yoked with unbelievers. For what fellowship has righteousness with lawlessness? And what communion has light with darkness?"* (2 Corinthians 6:14, NKJV)

We have openly and thoughtlessly allowed the infiltration of unlike spirits into the assembly of the body of Christ. In 1 Corinthians 5:6 Paul tell us that glorying is not good when allowing such spirits into the worship experience. He says, *"do you not know that a little leaven leavens the whole lump?"* As stated earlier, inviting unbelievers to church in itself is not the issue but not sharing Christ with them is where we are missing the church's purpose in the earth. It is obvious to most of us that there are more people attending church who have not made Christ their Lord and savior than those that have. I believe the Lord has inspired this message to acknowledge that the reason for this is because we are not handling the gospel in the way that we were commanded by Jesus.

This is again especially true in cultures where there is no authorized persecution for faith in Christ. Can we ourselves distinguish who is a true believer and who is not? No! The Lord has told us not to condemn for we do not know a man's heart. However, it is our purpose to be sure that these individuals have been given the true gospel in order for them to make an informed choice. Where we are failing is that we believe that we can transform an individual by allowing them to sing, pray, and serve within the body.

We have no power to transform a person's heart. This is God promise but we are to act as co-laborers in offering the power of salvation through the gospel of Christ.

Consider a team of employees working to complete a task in a timely manner. However, at least one member of the team is unequipped to help with the task. They haven't the knowledge, skill or desire to see this task completed. They talk well and perpetrate their abilities very convincingly, but without the necessary skills and abilities, they can cause the project to fail. It is this kind of infiltration that is spoken of when we allow and even encourage those who do not have the Spirit of God to participate in the ministry of the church. The things of the spirit can only be understood spiritually. *"But the natural man does not receive the things of the Spirit of God, for they are foolishness to him; nor can he know them, because they are spiritually discerned".* (1 Corinthians 2:14 (NKJV) It has been my experience and observation that few people become saved during these meetings. As a bible study teacher, when asked for testimonies, I have found that most believers are saved elsewhere and they come to the church to publicly acknowledge their faith in the Lord Jesus as savior and Lord of their lives. By no means is this writer suggesting that the church cannot have a gathering of believers and unbelievers with the hope of introducing them to Christ Jesus, however, this was once called a crusade. It was a call to unbelievers to be saved.

The church routinely invites the unsaved to worship services without the benefit of sharing the gospel with that person first. This is done often because of our slothfulness or insecurities. We make the decision to leave the sharing of the gospel to the minister. It is enough that we get them to church. There are many genuine worship services that do not specifically share the gospel at every service. If we continue to think that a man can be saved without the gospel, then it would seem that we are suggesting that God word is not true. The truth is, *"For God so loved the world that He gave His only begotten Son, so that whoever believes in Him should not perish but have everlasting life"* John 3:16 (NJKV). This is the provision that God has made for the salvation of man and it has not and will not change. That provision is called *Jesus Christ*! What eternal good does it do for man to join a church family without the seal of the Holy Spirit?

Always remembering that a man's eternal state is ultimately between that man and God, he seeks to direct the church back to the basics of presenting the true gospel and not participating in the enemies tactic of deceiving people into thinking they are saved when they do not have the Spirit of God.

Our first response to the love of God is to share that love with others by sharing the good news of salvation. We must be ready when the Holy Spirit gives us a command to tell people that God loves them and has sent his son, Jesus to pay their sin debt. This is the most important act of God's love we perform. We must go back to the *Acts* of the Apostles. It is there that we will find the church that Christ called into existence. The word *church* is defined as "a *community of believers* called out of the world." Jesus states in Matthew 15:16 that He would build his church on the confession of Peter. Consequently, Jesus builds the church, not man. In his infinite mercy, our Lord has seen fit to speak to us about this error.

> The foundation has been set, let us build on it.
> But let each one take heed how he builds on it.
> For no other foundation can anyone lay than that
> which is laid, which is Jesus Christ.
> 1 Corinthians 3:10-11 (RSV).

I encourage you to read the letters to the churches found in Revelation 2 and 3. While it is necessary for the church to adapt its ministries to the culture in which it exists, the church must never change the foundation of that ministry, no matter how the world changes.

The Promise of the Holy Spirit As Your Witness

> The Spirit Himself bears witness with our spirit
> that we are children of God, and if children, then
> heirs—heirs of God and joint heirs with Christ,
> if indeed we suffer with Him, that we may also be
> glorified together.
> Romans 8:16-17 (KJV)

Are you concerned that you are committing *identity theft* with the name of Jesus? If you are, one way to test your faith's authenticity is to ask yourself if you are saved. You do not have to ask anyone else. The Spirit of God will reveal to anyone their need for forgiveness or their acceptance of forgiveness through Jesus Christ when they seek to know. If you sincerely seek God, your answer can be yes without hesitation because the Holy Spirit of God will witness to your spirit that you are born again and a new creature in Christ Jesus. On the other hand, if you can not answer with an unequivocal yes, how freely our Lord will receive you into his family when you sincerely confess with your mouth the Lord Jesus and believe in your heart that God raised Him from the dead. You can then be confident that you know the Lord Jesus as your Lord and Savior and you can also be confident that the Lord Jesus knows you as a member of His body. This requires no other person. It is between you and the Lord Jesus, and He will affirm your salvation by the seal and witnessing of His Holy Spirit.

Consider the next two scenarios for clarification, the first will be hypothetical and the other will be my own experience. Let's suppose someone is alone and in a perilous situation. During this time, they are reminded by the Spirit of God of the hope of forgiveness through Jesus Christ shared with them by a friend, a loved one, or even a stranger at an earlier time in their life. They are now able to believe and pray the prayer of faith. At this moment the person is filled with the confidence that the Lord heard their prayer and they accept this forgiveness. This person later dies without the opportunity to tell anyone or receive any affirmation from another person. The Bible teaches that this person would be just as saved as the person who walked in God's grace for years.

My personal testimony is over year30 years ago I was alone in my bedroom when the Lord Jesus revealed Himself to me. After rejoicing in the awesome grace of God, the very same evening I called several friends and loved ones to tell them that I had been saved. The following Sunday I went to church to make a public acknowledgement. In either of these scenarios, the conversion was personal between the Lord Jesus and the person.

The gospel of Jesus Christ is the only gospel that has the power to lead a sinful man to a forgiving God. Paul tells us, *"For I am not ashamed of the gospel of Christ, for it is the power of God to salvation for everyone who believes"* (Romans 1:16, NKJV).

God has in these last days spoken to us by His son. He has kept His promise and sent to those who would believe the Spirit of truth to guide us into all truth and to glorify Christ. (John 16:13-14) Without the Spirit of God, could anyone believe in their heart that the creator of the heaven and the earth would love man so much that He would step down from heaven to dwell among sinful man, to be rebuked, accused, betrayed, humiliated, wounded, and bruised all for the salvation of a sinful creation while they were dead in their sins? At this time, a choice to accept or reject Christ as Lord and Savior is made. If this gift of grace is accepted, *the Holy Spirit, who is our guarantee of the inheritance, seals that person until the day of redemption of the purchased possession, to the praise of His glory* (Ephesians 1:14). This is the new birth and a new babe in Christ is born.

As with any baby, there must be someone who will care for, nurture, teach, and walk with that child in order for that baby to become a responsible adult. When there is a new birth within the church, it is the mature members of the body of Christ responsibility to be that person.

> Jesus tells us "Go therefore and make disciples of all the nations, baptizing them in the name of the Father and the Son and of the Holy Spirit, teaching them to observe all things that I have commanded you." Matthew 28:219-20 (NKJV)

Without that teaching and example, that new baby will not live an abundant life because he or she will not be able to enjoy and grow from the meat of God's word.

Jesus' Insurance Against Identity Theft

Jesus answered, "Most assuredly, I say to you,
unless one is born of water and the Spirit, he can
not enter the kingdom of God."
John 3:5 (RSV)

In the world, many creditors have developed identity theft insurance. For a price, you can protect yourself—not from identity theft, but from the consequences of identity theft. While it is possible for someone to steal your identity, this insurance will protect you from the responsibility of paying for items or services purchased or obtained by using your name without your permission.

Our Lord in his wisdom and omniscience has put into place insurance against benefiting from the use of His name without His permission. He has set a prerequisite to the using of His name for eternal benefits. This prerequisite is that *you must be born again to enter the kingdom of God.* While the name of Jesus can be stolen and used, he has no duty to allow these persons to receive the eternal or even the earthly benefits made available to all who use it.

In Genesis 3:24, we are told that when God put Adam and Eve out of the Garden of Eden, *"He placed cherubim at the east of the garden of Eden, and a flaming sword which turned every way to guard the way to the tree of life."* He did this so that they could not eat of the tree of life and live forever in their sinful state. In John 3:5-8, Jesus has done the same thing by saying, *"Unless a man is born again by the Spirit, he cannot see the kingdom of God"* (John 3:8, NKJV). This is the insurance that our Savior has put in place to protect what has been made available only for those who accept the lordship and saving grace of our Lord, Jesus Christ.

The compassion of God and His will that all come to the saving knowledge of Jesus Christ is expressed so plainly in this mandate. Yes, it can be confusing, as noted by Nicodemus, who was a teacher of the law. He asked Jesus, *"How can these things be? Can a man enter a second time his mother's womb and be born again?"* Jesus goes on to tell Him, *'The wind blows where it wishes, and you hear the sound of it, but cannot tell where it comes from and where it goes. So is everyone who is born of the Spirit"* (John 3:8, RSV).

The Bible sometimes refers to the church as the "bride of Christ." In light of this, I ask you to consider a marriage relationship. When a man and a woman make the vows of marriage, he and she consummate that marriage by coming together in intercourse. In this union, they become one flesh. *"Therefore a man shall leave his father and mother and be joined to his wife, and they shall become one flesh"* (Genesis 2:24, NKJV). It is at this time that the marriage vow is sealed. When a person makes a confession of faith in the Lord Jesus, that relationship is not validated or sealed until the Holy Spirit of God enters that person. *"But he who is joined to the Lord is one spirit with Him"* (1 Corinthians 6:17, NKJV). Jesus must be invited into the heart of that person. It is at this time that the person and Jesus become one. This is the insurance that Jesus has set in place so that only those who have been grafted into the family of God through grace can enter the kingdom of heaven.

Grace to Glory

Moreover, the law entered that the offense might abound. But where sin abounded, grace abounded much more, so that as sin reigned in death, even so grace might reign through righteousness to eternal life through Jesus Christ our Lord.
Romans 5:20-21(NKJV)

During the time that this book was being written, I had a dream. I will even call it a nightmare, because I have never felt such misery. I dreamed that I had an abortion. In this dream, the doctor told me that he had watched the head of the baby "who had bright eyes" go down the drain. When he said this, I was mortified. I cannot fully explain how I felt with words. However, I will say that I felt brokenhearted because it was after the doctor's statement that I became aware of what I had done. In this dream, I perceived that I had the same relationship with Jesus that I have now. In other words, I knew Him and was sure that He knew me. I delighted in the Lord as I do now.

My relationship with Christ contributed to my distress and broken heart. In the dream, I began to wail because I felt so separated from God. I could not understand how I could have done such a thing when I knew the Lord Jesus as I did. I felt that there was no way out of this, no way could I undo what I had done. The emotional pain was so intense that I woke my husband with the wailing. When I came to myself, I was thankful that it had only been a dream. Shortly afterwards I went back to sleep and dreamed that I was at the hospital preparing to have an abortion. In the dream, I was waiting for a vacant bed and was told to go into another room until one was available.

The next morning, I remembered the dreams and knew they represented something. I knew that the dreams were important because not once, but twice, I dreamed that I was having an abortion. As I pondered the dream, I could not get peace from any meanings that I tried to associate to them. After some time of trying to understand it, I went to the Lord and asked Him to please show me their meaning. I finished praying and forgot about the dreams, trusting that sooner or later, God would reveal it to me.

Later, as I was working on this book and reviewing what had already been written, I came across the passage:

> I trust that he will allow you to see that unless the church takes seriously the responsibility given it by the Lord Jesus, it will, without knowledge or intent, participate in the destruction of many who call themselves believers.

When I read this, the dream came back to me with the same original intensity. It became obvious that this was what the dream represented. The church is aborting "*bright-eyed*" babes by not giving them the gospel of Christ, which is the opportunity for life everlasting. We are causing people who might otherwise live in Christ to die because we have not shared with them the good news that God, the Father, sent Jesus, the Son, to pay man's sin debt. We have not told them that when they acknowledge their need for a savior, God then sends the Holy Spirit to dwell within their hearts, grafting them into the household of faith. Just as in the dream, we would never do this intentionally, and to realize we have done it causes an unbearable pain and sadness.

I then began to listen to the Lord concerning the dreams, and another purpose of the dream was shown to me: the sufficiency of the grace of God. I remember feeling condemned for my actions. I could not imagine the Lord forgiving me for this because I could not comprehend forgiveness for such a thing when I knew and trusted the Lord with all my heart. I realized that I could not expect the forgiveness of God because I could not forgive myself. I felt that my faith must have been lacking something, otherwise how could I willingly do such a thing as kill a *"bright-eyed"* baby? I felt totally separated from God.

I have taken my time and yours to share this with you so that anyone who is reading this and feels that they have done things that cannot be forgiven will know that God's grace is sufficient. This has also been included for the church to know that even though we have fallen short in our commission to share the true gospel of Jesus Christ, it is *not* too late. God's throne of grace is where we can come for mercy and for grace to help in this time of need (Hebrews 4:16, NKJV).

Let us rejoice in the knowledge that *"There is therefore now no condemnation to those who are in Christ Jesus who do not walk according to the flesh, but according to the Spirit"* (Romans 8:1, NKJV). This plan for salvation was prepared before the foundation of the world by a sovereign and omniscient God. The enemies (the world, the flesh, and Satan) cannot use sin to stop what God has started in those who are sealed with the Holy Spirit. Where there is sin, there is grace for the children of God. The bigger the sin, the greater the grace. The greater the grace, the brighter the glory of God. Remember this is not a license to sin, but it is encouragement to know that should you sin, the grace of God is sufficient and the glory of God is manifested.

Summary

Let us now search our hearts and be sure that we have willingly invited the Lord Jesus into our hearts as the Lord and Savior of our lives, not just because we have heard of Him, but because we have heard and believed. Let us examine ourselves and be sure that we have received the gift of the Holy Spirit, not accepting it to be so because of our emotions or feelings but because of faith. It is by faith that the just should live, not by emotions or feelings. Let us be careful to accept the Lord Jesus as Lord of our lives and not just Savior.

We must not just believe *in* Christ, but we must believe *upon* Christ. Believing *in* Christ is not enough. Believing in someone does not automatically make you a follower of that person. It only says that you believe that they are who they say they are. Therefore, you cannot experience an oneness with them. However, when you believe *on* someone, it is suggested that you depend on this person respective to your need. Furthermore, your choices and actions are usually based on that belief.

I implore all who read this to stop and take this moment to examine your relationship with our Savior. Does Jesus know you? Has this relationship been consummated? Has His Spirit joined with your spirit? Do you love Him because He loved you first? When you can answer with an emphatic *yes* to these questions, you will no longer hesitate when someone ask if you are saved from the wrath of God.

I implore the genuine believer to take care to listen to the Spirit of God when obeying the unction to share the gospel with the unsaved. Lead them to Christ by sharing the gospel of Christ, *then* bring them to church for fellowship. Remember we are to be holy (different) than the world, for our God is holy. Let us be careful not to conform to the world and its system, but be transformed by the renewing of our minds. Let us not be so concerned with church growth but instead trust Christ to multiply His church as the Spirit wills.

The Lord is calling for the whole church to begin by the power and anointing of the Holy Spirit to share the true gospel of Christ to unbelievers and trust in the power of God to use his gospel to bring people out of darkness into his marvelous light. I believe that sometimes we become so comfortable in our relationships with Christ that we take for granted the spiritual state of others. This is especially true when this person is nice and seemingly good. We can fellowship with people for years and one day find out they never heard the gospel presented to them. They can be in church every Sunday and participating in all the church activities and/or ministries but they have never accepted Christ as Lord and savior. I have heard the testimonies of some of these people. How can this be possible except that we take a person's spiritual state for granted based on their works? The community of believers who have been called out of the world must not conform to the world in its methods to get people into the church. The church must simply be holy and obedient to the Spirit of God and *"the Lord will add to the church daily those who are being saved"* (Acts 2:47, NKJV), just as He did in the early church. One practical way the church can be the light of God that draws men and the salt of the earth that preserves the world is to stop focusing so much on organized programs and began focusing more on living individual lives unto the Lord. In other words, make sincere and purposeful efforts for daily walks in faith and not just Sunday or Wednesday walks of faith. The world needs to see practical acts of faith and not just organized acts of faith.

Most of us know people who wear the title of Christian but otherwise live consistently empty and defeated lives. An empty life is one in which there is no eternal purpose for living. Living defeated lives means living according to the world's system. It's living life in hopelessness or putting hope and trust in man and earthly riches to give peace and security which only leads to defeat. It has become so easy to ignore this state in our friends and family. This happens because we accept the lie that the enemy has planted. He has deceived us into thinking that we are showing God's love when we turn a blind eye to people in this condition. This is not an expression of God's love but an expression of our fear of rejection and our irresponsibility as laborers for the Lord of the harvest.

I encourage you by reminding you that we do not have to fear rejection or ridicule. Jesus says,

> If the world hates you, you know that it hated me
> before it hated you. If you were of the world, the
> world would love its own. Yet because you are not
> of the world, but I chose you out of the world,
> therefore the world hates you.
> John 15:18-19 (NKJV)

I am compelled to pray today that the Lord of the harvest will send bold, Spirit filled laborers into his harvest.

Scriptures to Consider

Matthew 7: 21-23	Parable of the Sheep and Goat
Matthew 13:18-23	Parable of the Sower
Matthew 16:15-20	Confession of Faith
Matthew 22-1-14	Parable of the Wedding Feast
Matthew 25:1-13	Parable of the Wise and Foolish Virgins
John 16	Promise of the Holy Spirit
1 Corinthians 2:9-16	Spiritual Understanding
1 Corinthians 13	God's Love
Galatians 5:24-25	Living by the Spirit
Galatians 6:7-8	Reaping What You Sow
Ephesians 4:11-27	Spiritual Gifts are for Believers